THE HUGE AND HORRIBLE BEAST

and other stories

Sean Taylor

Illustrated by

Tim Archbold

OXFORD
UNIVERSITY PRESS

OXFORD
UNIVERSITY PRESS

Great Clarendon Street, Oxford OX2 6DP

Oxford University Press is a department of the University of Oxford.
It furthers the University's objective of excellence in research, scholarship,
and education by publishing worldwide in

Oxford New York

Auckland Cape Town Dar es Salaam Hong Kong Karachi
Kuala Lumpur Madrid Melbourne Mexico City Nairobi
New Delhi Shanghai Taipei Toronto

With offices in

Argentina Austria Brazil Chile Czech Republic France Greece
Guatemala Hungary Italy Japan South Korea Poland Portugal
Singapore Switzerland Thailand Turkey Ukraine Vietnam

Oxford is a registered trade mark of Oxford University Press
in the UK and in certain other countries

First published 2003

British Library Cataloguing in Publication Data

Data available

ISBN-13: 978-0-19-919614-2
ISBN-10: 0-19-919614-1

5 7 9 10 8 6

Mixed Pack (1 of 6 different titles): ISBN 0 19 919616 8
Class Pack (6 copies of 6 titles): ISBN 0 19 919615 X

Printed in China by Imago

Contents

The Huge and Horrible Beast

A story from Brazil

Once there was a lad from a little farm on the Brazilian plains. His name was Zé.

Zé was bored with the quiet life on the farm. So, one day, he told his mother and father that he was going off into the big wide world to seek his fortune.

His father looked a little worried.

You see, Zé was brave and warm-hearted, but he was not very clever. If you had asked him what 3 times 8 was, he would probably have said, "Twelve."

And if you had asked him how to spell "EXTRAORDINARY", he would have tried his best, but got it completely wrong.

So his father felt he ought to give him some wise advice. He scratched his head.

Then he said, "Zé, my son, remember this. If you find anything on your way, pick it up and keep it. It might come in handy later."

"That's wise advice," nodded Zé, "I shall remember it."

Then he kissed his mother, hugged his father and off he went.

He took the track across the plains until he reached fields and forests that he had never seen before.

And, as he walked through one of the forests, he came across a great, long, twisty length of creeper lying on the path in front of him.

"Dad told me that if I find anything on my way I'm to pick it up and keep it," he said to himself.

So he picked up the twisty creeper, coiled it several times around his waist and walked on.

He crossed rivers and valleys that he had never even heard of.

At the end of one of the valleys, Zé came across a metal gate. It was so old that it had fallen off its hinges and was lying on the ground.

"Dad told me that if I found anything on my way I should pick it up," he said to himself.

So he picked up the metal gate, slung it over his shoulder and walked on.

He reached lakes and hills that he had never even imagined. And, as he started up one of the hills a small, pink pig came waddling across the path in front of him.

"Dad told me that if I found anything on my way then I should pick it up," he said to himself.

So he picked up the pig, tucked it under his arm and walked on.

It was getting dark and Zé was more than a little bit tired. So he decided to find a place to spend the night.

About halfway up the hill there was a small house. He thought he would ask if he could spend the night there.

There was a gaggle of hungry-looking children playing in the garden.

They stopped and stared when they saw Zé walking up their path with a creeper wrapped around his waist, a gate over his shoulder, and a pig under one arm.

Then they burst into giggles.

The children's mother looked out of the window to see what was happening. Zé gave her a cheerful smile.

"Good evening, Madam," he said. "I'm travelling in search of my fortune and I need somewhere to stay the night."

"Well," said the woman, "I am a poor widow with seven hungry children. There's barely enough room for us in this small house. All I can offer you is our big, black hay-barn at the top of this hill …"

"That would do just fine," said Zé.

"But," went on the widow, "there is one problem."

"Oh, yes?" said Zé.

“It’s a very big problem,” said one of the girls.

“Yes,” said the widow, “A huge and horrible beast lives in that hay-barn.”

“It’s been up there for as long as anyone can remember,” said the girl.

“No one knows why,” added her brother.

“But if anyone goes in that barn, they never come back alive,” said another boy.

"All I'm going to do is curl up in the hay," said Zé, "I don't think I'll bother the huge and horrible beast, if there really is one. So I am going to take you up on your offer."

"Good luck, then," said the widow. But she had a worried frown. Zé seemed such a nice, friendly young man.

"I'll see you in the morning," said Zé and off he went, striding up the hill.

The big, black door opened with a low creak.

Zé walked in, put down his things and stretched out in the hay for a good night's sleep.

But, no sooner had he laid down his head than there was a sound from above him in the loft.

Something heavy was moving.

Zé opened his eyes and a deep voice boomed in the darkness.

Zé closed his eyes again and tried to ignore the voice.

"I AM A HUGE AND HORRIBLE BEAST," came the voice again.

"Well, so am I," said Zé.

There was a moment's silence.

"WHAT?" came the voice.

"I said, SO AM I," said Zé. "Now keep your voice down. I'm trying to get some sleep."

“YOU’RE A HUGE AND HORRIBLE BEAST TOO?” said the voice.

“Yes,” said Zé.

“THEN PASS ME UP … ONE OF YOUR HAIRS!”

Zé thought for a moment.

Then he undid the twisty creeper wrapped around his waist. He passed it up through the opening into the loft.

“OH,” said the voice. “THAT’S ONE OF YOUR HAIRS?”

“Yes, that’s one of my hairs,” said Zé.

“MMM,” said the voice. “THEN SHOW ME … YOUR COMB.”

“All right,” said Zé.

And he passed the gate up through the opening into the loft.

"THAT'S YOUR COMB?" said the voice.

"Yes. That's my comb," said Zé.

"MMM," said the voice. "WELL … THEN, SHOW ME … ONE OF YOUR NITS!"

"All right," said Zé, and he passed up the pig.

"THAT'S ONE OF YOUR NITS?" came the voice from upstairs, sounding rather scared.

"That's one of my nits," said Zé.

"YOU REALLY **ARE** A HUGE AND HORRIBLE BEAST THEN," boomed the voice.

"That's right," nodded Zé.

Next thing, there was a shuffling of heavy feet upstairs.

Then came the creak of a window opening, a loud thud, and the sound of something pounding off down the other side of the hill.

“That’s got rid of *him,*” yawned Zé. “I knew my dad’s advice was wise.”

He was about to close his eyes and go to sleep. But then he felt a little curious to find out what the huge and horrible beast had been doing for all those years, up in the loft.

So he pushed a ladder into the opening, climbed up, and what should he find there but a big chest?

Inside the chest, what should there be but hundreds and hundreds of golden coins?

The huge and horrible beast didn't come back. So, in the morning, Zé took the chest of gold and gave it to the poor widow and her hungry children.

The poor widow was delighted to find out that she was rather a rich widow.

She gave a big bag of gold coins to Zé.

So Zé went home with a fortune in his bag.

And perhaps he used the money to go to night school and learn his eight times table and how to spell "EXTRAORDINARY" …

And perhaps he didn't.

The Milkman and the Monkey

A story from India

Some time ago, in a certain town in India – whose name I know but will keep to myself – there was a milkman.

He made his living by travelling around the town with two silver pans full of milk.

"BEST MILK! CREAMY MILK!" he would shout.

"WHITE AS SNOW! SMOOTH AS SILK!"

When they heard his call, the people of the town would come out with their wooden bowls.

The milkman would take a coin from each of them and drop the money into his old coin-bag.

Then he would carefully fill their bowls with milk.

He was a clever little man. He always managed to get hold of milk, even when the other milkmen had run out.

And, at the end of the day, you could hear the money clinking and jingling in his coin-bag.

But everything was not as it seemed with this milkman.

You see, early in the morning, on his way to sell the milk, he used to stop at a well.

He would look carefully around him. Then he would wind a bucketful of water up from the bottom of the well and slip the water into his pans of milk.

So the milk he sold was only *half* milk. And that way he got twice the amount of money he deserved.

The milkman thought he was pretty clever doing this.

The villagers were simple, honest people. And, if the milk sometimes tasted a bit thin, they would just shake their heads and say, "The cows are drinking a lot of water in this hot weather!"

An old monkey lived in the trees above the well.

If ever the milkman caught sight of her he would hiss, "Shoo! Gedoutofit you stupid old BANANA-HEAD!"

The monkey would scamper up into the top branches of the tree.

But she would keep her pale eyes on the milkman, as he wound the bucket up from the bottom of the well.

One day, it was so hot that you could almost cut the air with a knife.

The little milkman stopped at the well in the morning. Then he shooed away the monkey and, as usual, watered down his milk.

It was one of the milkman's good days.

He sold every single drop of his milk and ended up with one hundred coins in his bag.

It was so hot that he stopped at the well for a drink on his way home.

He put down his coin-bag and wound up a bucket of cool water.

In the tree above him, the old monkey blinked.

Then, as the bucket squeaked up, she began to swing softly down through the branches.

The milkman cupped his hands in the water. Behind him, the old monkey dropped with a dusty thud to the ground.

She reached out a bony finger and hooked it round the strap of the coin-bag.

The milkman turned round.

His coin-bag wasn't there!

His mouth fell open.

"Thieves, THIEVES!" he screeched.

Then he heard a tiny little jingle from above him. He looked up, and you know what he saw: the monkey, with the coin-bag in her hand.

"EH!" pointed the milkman, "Give me that! That's mine! You knock-kneed, flea-bitten, NUMBSKULL!"

The monkey blinked.

"I SAID, GIVE IT BACK!" yelled the milkman, trying to grab the monkey by her tail.

But the monkey reached a crooked paw into the bag, took out a coin and flicked it into the air.

The coin winked for a moment in the sunshine, then tumbled into the darkness of the well.

PLINK!

“What are you doing, you cloth-eared, armpit-scratching, SPONGE-BRAIN?” yelled the milkman, looking around for a stick or a stone to throw at the monkey. “THAT’S MONEY, THAT IS!”

But the monkey fished out another coin and flicked it after the first.

“NO!” bellowed the milkman, clutching his head and stamping his feet, “STOP IT!”

But the monkey did not stop. She carried on and on until twenty … thirty … forty … FIFTY silver coins had gone glinting down into the well.

The milkman was down on his knees. He was holding out his hands.

He was begging the monkey to stop.

And suddenly the monkey dropped the coin-bag.

The little man scrambled through the dust and grabbed at his money.

"Half of it's gone," he whimpered.

The monkey blinked, as if to say, "Half of the milk you sold was water. So half of the money belongs down that well."

The milkman hung his head. Suddenly he felt ashamed.

He had thought he was the clever one, tricking people with his watery milk. But now the old monkey up in the tree had made him look a fool.

And, you know, from that day he never mixed water into his milk again.

In fact, the milk he sold was the best for miles around. It really was white as snow and smooth as silk.

Everyone wanted to buy it.

And that's why I am not going to tell you the name of the village he came from.

Because if everyone went there to buy his milk, there wouldn't be enough for the simple, honest people of the town.

The Clever Hunter and the Elephant

A story from the Bakongo people of Central Africa

Long ago there was a clever hunter. He knew a hundred crafty ways to catch animals.

One day, he went deep into the forest and dug a deep hole in the ground. Then he covered it with branches, leaves and sand.

The next morning he came back with his spear to see if anything had fallen into the hole.

He was delighted to find he had caught a great big elephant.

The hunter hopped from foot to foot because he had been so clever.

Then he looked down at the animal in the hole and said, “Ah! Elephant! You fell right for it! This trap was easy enough to see! It was your stupidity that brought you here!”

The old elephant blinked his watery, brown eyes and said, "It *was* my stupidity that brought me here. You're right. But I'll tell you something, hunter. Your cleverness will bring you here too."

The hunter was flabbergasted.

"An elephant that talks!" he said. "Who has ever caught a talking elephant before? This will prove I am the cleverest hunter that ever lived!"

The hunter hurried back to his village and went straight to the Chief.

"What do you want, little hunter?" asked the Chief's guards.

"Let me see the Chief!"

"The Chief is busy."

"But I have news he must hear."

"What sort of news?"

"News that will amaze and delight him."

The guards did not look impressed. But one of them nodded and led the hunter inside.

The Chief was talking to a group of village elders and he was not best pleased to be disturbed.

"Well, hunter?" he said. "What's this news? It had better be worth hearing."

"It is," said the hunter. "I have done something very clever indeed. I have caught an elephant that talks!"

The Chief stared at the hunter for a moment. Then he threw back his head and roared with laughter.

"Don't waste my time, you liar!" he said. "There is no such thing as an elephant that talks!"

"There is, sir," said the hunter, "I talked to it just as I am talking to you. It is in a trap in the forest. Come with me and I will show you."

“I’m busy,” sighed the Chief.

“Every day you are busy,” said the hunter. “But not every day you have the chance to talk to an elephant.”

The Chief thought for a moment.

Then he got to his feet with a very stern stare and said, “This had better be the truth.”

"If it is a lie I will move from this village," said the hunter. "If you do not see an elephant that talks, I promise to go and live right there in the forest where I leave my traps."

"I shall remember your words," said the Chief, "Now let's go."

The hunter led the way into the forest.

When they reached the trap, there was the elephant, slowly shifting his feet in the hole.

"There he is!" said the hunter.

The hunter walked up to the hole and said, "Elephant! You in that trap! It was your stupidity that brought you here!"

The elephant gave a soft sniff with his trunk, but said nothing.

"Do you hear me?" smiled the hunter. "I said it was your stupidity that brought you here!"

The elephant flapped a dusty ear, but said nothing.

"Hey!" said the hunter, prodding the elephant with his spear. "It was your stupidity that brought you here!"

The elephant blinked slowly, but said nothing.

A scowl spread over the Chief's face.

"Hunter, you're a time-waster and a liar!" he said. "This elephant is no different from any other! Remember your promise? I will make sure you keep it! Collect your things from the village! From now on you are going to live right here in the forest!"

The hunter knew there was no arguing with the Chief. He collected his possessions, said goodbye to his friends and made his way back to the forest.

When he reached the trap, he called down to the elephant, "You foolish animal! Why didn't you speak?"

And, this time, the elephant spoke.

"It was my stupidity that brought *me* here," he said. "But it was your cleverness that brought *you* here. One of us was foolish. The other was clever. But we have ended up in the same place!"

And ever since, there has been a saying in Africa: "Too foolish and too clever, they are brothers!"

Why the Lion and the Hare are Not the Best of Friends

A story from Tibet

The lion was feeling hungry. He looked about and spotted a hare nibbling grass on the side of the hill.

The lion crept slowly through the grass. The hare was munching away at the stalks and she didn't notice the lion until it was too late.

A great hairy paw grabbed her.

"Oooh," squealed the hare, "I didn't see you there, Lion! What are you doing?"

"I think I will probably EAT YOU," growled the lion.

"You will find me very small and bony!" squeaked the hare.

"You look like a rather tasty little snack to me," growled the lion.

"I know where you can find a much bigger meal," said the hare. "I know where you can find an animal as big as you!"

The lion paused.

"As big as me?"

"Yes."

"That would be a very nice snack."

"It isn't far away either," added the hare.

"Mmm," thought the lion.

"All right. Show me this place. But if you try to run off I'll grab you and swallow you down without even chewing!"

The lion loosened his claws and the hare hopped out of his paw.

Then she led him down the hill to a lake. When she got to the edge, she nodded into the water.

"Look," said the hare. "There it is."

The lion looked into the water and what do you think he saw?

He saw an animal just his size.

And, what's more, when he growled, it growled back. When he snarled, it snarled back. And when he roared, it roared back.

The lion felt irritated with the rude animal in the lake. So he swiped a paw at it. And it swiped a paw back! That was just too much.

In a rage, the lion leapt at his own reflection.

Down he splashed into the cold, murky water.

That was how the hare escaped.

And that is why the lion and the hare are not exactly the best of friends.

About the author

I have been lucky enough to travel to many different countries. I now spend some of my life in England, and some of it in Brazil, where my wife comes from. In 1990 I met a storyteller called Duncan Williamson. He invited me to a storytelling get-together *(a ceilidh)* in his house in Scotland. That was when I started telling stories myself. And, ever since, I have listened out for good tales wherever I go.